Reflections Within

A Free Verse Poetry Collection

Lora C Mercado

© 2014 by Lora C. Mercado

Reflections Within - A Free Verse Poetry Collection
ISBN: 978-0991026999

Author photo courtesy of Joseph Ciarrochi

Marguerite Publishing
www.margueritepublishing.com

Table of Contents

Table of Contents

Introduction

The poems in this book are raw, spiritual, deep and very personal. You will find happiness, despair and many memories within these pages. We all have similar situations in our lives, and I hope that these words will resonate with your spirit.

Enjoy…

~ Lora Mercado

Reflections Within

A Free Verse Poetry Collection

Lora C Mercado

Lotus

Emerging from the waters
As the sun begins to rise
The beauty is astounding
Then descending
At night fall
Deep into the pond
Into the darkness
But always starting anew
Rising up again
I can learn a lot from you

Rainbow

Does the rainbow lead to you?
I see it after the storm
In the heavens, your spirit lives
In my arms you are no more
My heart aches and is empty
I wish you had never gone
My son, I will love you forever

My Beauty

Full of life and love
My little beauty
You are a gift
My gift
Delicate fingers
Brown curly locks
A heart of gold
The sweetness of sugar
My daughter
My beauty
My love has no end

Hold On

Hold on little birdies
Hold on
The winds are much too strong
Rain pelting the nest
Mother shelters from the storm
Hold on little birdies
Hold on

Same

Cut from the same cloth
Yet polar opposites
You see black
I see white
It is all the same
But we have never agreed

Judgment

Who are you to judge?
Everyone is different
Even you
You are no better than me
You are no better than them
The ones you dislike
The ones you are afraid of
The ones who are different
Different than you
Different ones have gifts
Beautiful Gifts
Gifts you will never know
Gifts you deny yourself
You judge now
But nobody handed you the gavel

Shower

The quietest place in the house
The sound of the water
Heat soothing muscles
A place to think
A place for solitude
A place to wash it away
A place to start the day
Start new
Start clean
Pray in the peace
Be still in the peace
But be sure to lock the door!

Coffee

My morning friend
It is hard to wake without you
Your scent is like no other
I pour you in my cup
Cream and sugar please
The first sip
Magic to my mouth
Companion on quiet mornings
Sunrise is the best
Always nearby
Now I can start my day

Selfish

You stripped me of my youth
And robbed me of happiness
Happiness that any child deserves
Maybe you forgave yourself
But I will struggle with forgiveness
Until my last breath
Selfish is what you were
Never thinking of the repercussions
Role model you were not
I learned on my own
How to live my life
Without your help
Without your presence
Without who you should have been

Shadow

Black cat
Pure love
Snuggles and purrs
Patient and sweet
Bedtime cuddles
Lull me to sleep
He has seen me struggle
He has seen me succeed
Many years with my Shadow
Always comforting me

Soft Cat

Soft white fur under my fingertips
Random patterns of gray
The purring soothes my spirit
I feel comfort in the warmth
Little kitty I saved your life
And also you saved mine

Art

Release your emotions
Your inner thoughts
Grab a brush
A guitar
A pen
A needle and thread
Just grab something
Let it all out
You can do it
We all can do it
Try it
You will be free

Abandoned

I was abandoned
Not on the church steps
Just abandoned
Didn't have to be
Bad choices were made
Priorities were skewed
Left to grow up quick
Quicker than I should
On my own
No boundaries
No guidance
But why?
Why was I not first?
First on your list
Others came before me
Left in the shadows
Running wild
Wilder than I should have
Had you been there
Been there to care for me
Instead of leaving me
Abandoned

Something Magical

Is it serendipity?
Coincidence or fate?
The moment you fall in love
When you discover
That your heart is full
Your life is complete
You know this is for real
Truly something magical
Hold on to that moment
Savor every second
Keep the world out of it
Concentrate on each other
Respect and kindness are key
Preserve this feeling
It is something to cherish
Some are not so lucky

Beach

Sink into the sand
Eyes closed
Listen to the sounds
Waves lapping
Children playing
Seagulls calling
Feel the warmth
Skin hot to the touch
Mind is clearing
It is noisy
Yet incredibly peaceful

Alone

I need to be alone
To gather my thoughts
To have space
To breathe
I need to be alone
To create
To relax
To forget
I need to be alone
So I can be myself
By myself
Alone

The Crystal

Stunning and powerful
Radiating energy
Beautiful
Calming
Ancient granter of wishes
What do you desire?
Tell it to the crystal
Set your intentions
Watch what unfolds
Use only for good
Protection and love
The crystal is charged
From the energy above

Nepotism

Running rampant
Through the family tree
It continues on
Never skipping a generation
How would it feel
To be on the other side?
It is bleak from where I stand
Never to be the Golden Child
Only the Black Sheep
Never coddled
Though I didn't need to be
Always strong
I am
And will always be

Fake

Always pretending to be
Someone that you are not
Trying to act like others
So you fit in
Be yourself
Stop being fake
You have been that way
Since I can remember
I get angry
Because I don't even know
Who the hell you are
Do you?

Anxiety

Morning
Eyes open
Feeling nervous
Worried
Will something bad happen?
Keep busy
Maybe it will go away
Ignore it
Maybe it will go away
But only for a moment
A breath of fresh air
Then it comes back
Comes back to rule me
Anxiety
Why did you choose me?
Or did I choose you?

Candle

Heavenly connection
Powerful flame
Flickering shapes
Hypnotic
Beautiful
Enchanting
Cathartic
I light this candle
For you

Sweet Sister

Oh how I wish I knew you
Had you not gone before me
I would not exist
Had you not come first
Had you not died
I often wonder if you
Would be like me
If we would be friends
A tight sister bond
That does not break
I pray for you every night
I know you watch over me
Even though we never met
My sweet sister.
I miss you
Though I do not know you

Tears

Tears fall easily
When you have been hurt
At times they refuse to fall
When you have been hurt
A sign of weakness?
I think not
They have to fall
Let out the sadness
Frustration
Guilt
Release the grief
Cry
Let it out
Being strong is hard
Holding back tears is hard
Let it go
Relief will come
When tears fall easily

In the Mirror

Sad eyes
Many flaws
Beautiful?
I don't believe it
Getting older
Makes it worse
More flaws
Finding new ones
With every look
In the mirror
It shouldn't matter
But it does
To me
I will never be
What I want to be
On the outside
What a shame
To not be happy
With what I see
In the mirror

Chapters of My Life

I look back
On the chapters of my life
Who I was
Who I have become
Grown over time
From the happy little girl
To innocence lost
Many broken hearts
Even more broken promises
Holding my sons lifeless body
Stands out the most
Precious times with my daughter
Saved me from ruin
Now she is growing older
New chapters will start again
I can only hope for a happy ending
To the chapters of my life

Hawk

You fly above me
Showing me your presence
You appear
When I am feeling weak
I cannot help to believe
You are my spirit guide
Helping me on my path
My path of life
Where my destiny lies
You encourage me
Inspire me
Comfort me
You amazing creature
I honor you
And I thank you

Graveyard

Old tombstones of the past
Ornate yet dilapidated
Who is buried there?
Why did they die?
History unknown
Curiosity fills my mind
So many children
In the ground below
Families torn apart by illness
Soldiers of war
I acknowledge you
Hoping you rest in peace
One day I will join you
Then others will wonder
About me

Pictures

Preserving moments
Click the camera
A millisecond in time
Captured on film
For years to come
People
Places
Objects
Nature
Never limited
Beauty is everywhere

Lipstick

Your anger
Will never be hidden
By the lipstick
You don't fool me

Harsh words
Will never be unsaid
By the lipstick
You don't fool me

Malicious behavior
Will never be hidden
By the lipstick
You don't fool me

I know who you are
Nothing will hide it
Nothing
Not even Lipstick

Ice

You shook the ice in your glass
Expecting another drink
Handed to you on demand
As the demons came out
From your broken down soul
It controlled you
Controlled the family
Then it killed you
Slowly
Painfully
It killed your spirit
It killed your body
The strong man was gone
Weaker from the drink
Oh why did they
Pour the bottle
Over the ice
In your glass
That you shook?

Liar

If you are told a lie
It hurts
If you tell a lie
It hurts
Everyone lies
Tiny lies
Earth shattering lies
Living with a lie
Is harder than truth
Stop lying
Be honest
For yourself
For others
Lies hurt

Blanket

Tiny baby
Wrapped in her blanket
Soft and warm

Little toddler
Dragging her blanket
Soft and dirty

Sweet one
Snuggling her blanket
Soft and secure

Cloud

White and fluffy
In the sky
Changing shape
Always transforming
Moving
Filling with rain
Turning gray
Releasing to the earth
Then moving on
Transforming again

Before I was a Mother

Before I was a mother
I didn't know
The true meaning
Of love
Of sacrifice
Who I am today
Is different
Than who I used to be

Before I was a mother
Self was priority
Now there is
No time for self
But that's ok
I give my all
To my child
Holding no regrets

Before I was a mother
I was naïve
I didn't know
The most beautiful gift
Is to hold your child
Look into their eyes
Feeling the bond of love
That God created

Grandmothers

One grandmother taught me to sew
One grandmother taught me about God
Both influencing my life
In positive ways

I remember being a child
Sitting with my grandmother
The creative one
Showing me photos

In her tiny albums
In her simple house
Her joys were simple
Like her home

Surprising me
With carefully made doll dresses
I still have those dresses
Each and every one

I remember being a child
Sitting with my grandmother
The religious one
Listening to her accent

She was from the south
Her house was big
She had nice things
I thought she was rich

Surprising me
With homemade cheese crackers
I still have that recipe
But I wish she was here to make it

Free

Running
Skipping
Playing
Dancing in the sprinkles
Jumping in puddles
No cares in the world
My little one
So carefree
So undamaged
From this crazy world
I hold these moments
Close to my heart
And pray
That she always
Feels so free

Time

Dictator of life
It eludes me
I thought I had plenty
But it is ticking by
So very quickly
I was just a child
How did I get here?
Please slow down
I am not ready
To be finished
With my time

Mommy

You know my secrets
You know where I have been
Yet you still love me
Never giving up on me
Always encouraging my ideas
I learned a lot from you
We struggled together
We made it through
Now mature
We can grow together
But you will always
Be Mommy to me

Dreams

Scattered thoughts
Sometimes with a plot
Who are these people?
Oh, "Hi! I know you!"

Strange yet familiar
Places you go
Traveling instantly
From scene to scene

Unusual
Sometimes falling
Pulling out teeth
Running in slow motion

Passionate kisses
The plot thickens…
Beep!
Time to wake up!

White Feathers

Appearing at random
At just the right time
I know it is you
Giving me a gift
My son from heaven
My little angel
A piece of your wing
To give me strength
To live my life
Without you

<u>Be sure to check out these other titles by Lora C Mercado:</u>

Our Angels Await, Stories of Love from Beyond
http://www.amazon.com/dp/B00FIV93OA

Oh Cheese! Homestyle Cheesy Favorites
http://www.amazon.com/dp/B00J3Y77TG

Tasteful Memories, A Collection of Family Comfort Food Recipes
http://www.amazon.com/dp/B00IPMF64K

Gimme That Chocolate! A PMS Survival Cookbook
http://www.amazon.com/dp/B00IT63L8U

Bunch O' Brunch
http://www.amazon.com/dp/B00JGYBV3Q

A Bundle of Yum
http://www.amazon.com/dp/B00JLLY74Y

Departed, A Collection of Historical Cemetery Photography
http://www.amazon.com/dp/B00GEE2CRA

Thank you for reading this book. If you have enjoyed it, please post a review on Amazon.
Thanks!

Lora

www.ingramcontent.com/pod-product-compliance
Lightning Source LLC
Chambersburg PA
CBHW021147020426
42331CB00005B/939